Children of
HAWAII

THE WORLD'S CHILDREN

Children of
HAWAII

written and photographed by
FRANK STAUB

Carolrhoda Books, Inc./Minneapolis

For the children of Hawaii, and for my friend Mary Ann.

Thanks to the Hawaii State Parks, Hilton Waikoloan Resort, Holualoa Elementary School, Keakealani Outdoor Education Center, National Park Service, Panaewa Rainforest Zoo, Puna Geothermal Energy Venture, Punaluu Beach County Park, Richardson Ocean Park, all those who appear in this book, and all those who helped make it possible.

Carolrhoda Books, Inc., The Lerner Publishing Group
241 First Avenue North, Minneapolis, MN U.S.A.

Website address: www.lernerbooks.com

LIBRARY OF CONGRESS CATALOGING-IN-PUBLICATION DATA

Staub, Frank
    Children of Hawaii / Frank Staub.
      p.   cm. — (World's children)
    Includes index.
    Summary: Introduces the history, geography, and culture of the island of Hawaii through the daily lives of children who live there.
    ISBN 1-57505-253-9
    1. Hawaii—Social life and customs—Juvenile literature.
  2. Children—Hawaii—Social life and customs—Juvenile literature.
  [1. Hawaii—Social life and customs.] I. Title. II. Series: World's children (Minneapolis, Minn.)
  DU624.5.S73 1999   98-15097
  996.9'1–dc21

Manufactured in the United States of America
1 2 3 4 5 6 – JR – 04 03 02 01 00 99

Hawaii is a unique place in many ways. Of all the United States of America, it is the only one made up entirely of islands. Hawaii alone lies completely in the tropics. And it is the only state that once had its own kings and queens.

The 132 islands that make up Hawaii lie in the middle of the Pacific Ocean. They form the northern part of a large island group called Polynesia.

Most of the Hawaiian Islands are very small, but eight of the islands are large. They are Niihau, Kauai, Oahu, Molokai, Lanai, Kahoolawe, Maui, and Hawaii.

In this book, you will meet children who live on the island for which the state is named—the island of Hawaii. Hawaii is almost twice as big as all of the other Hawaiian Islands combined. It is usually called the Big Island.

The first Hawaiians worshipped many gods and goddesses. These statues of gods were built by modern-day Hawaiians to remember their ancestors.

This historical park displays smaller versions of the canoes in which Polynesians traveled to Hawaii.

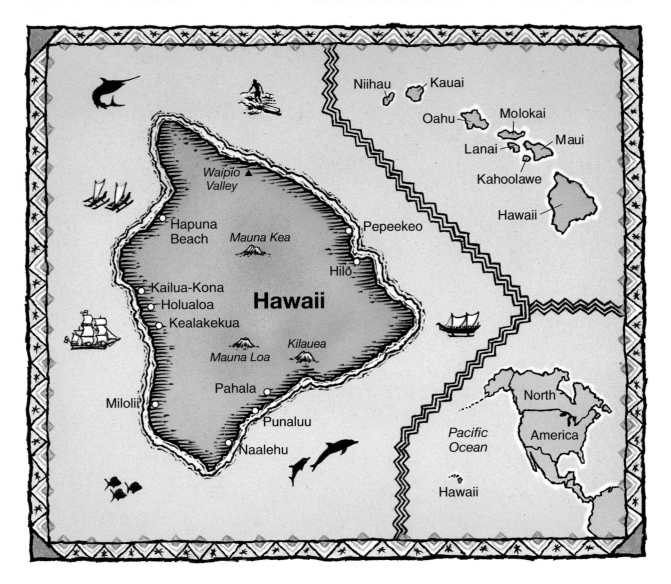

The first Hawaiians were Polynesians. They came from various western Pacific Islands about 2,000 years ago. They traveled to Hawaii in huge 80-foot-long canoes. Around A.D. 1200, Polynesians from the island of Tahiti arrived on the Big Island and conquered the first group of settlers. These early Hawaiians caught fish in the sea and raised fish in ponds. They also raised crops, pigs, and chickens.

Located near the northeastern coast of the Big Island, Akaka Falls is one of the highest waterfalls in the United States. It drops 442 feet.

Volcanoes began forming the Hawaiian Islands about 30 million years ago. Thick, red-hot liquid called lava flowed from cracks in the ocean floor. As the lava cooled, it hardened and formed mountains. Over time, as more lava flowed from volcanoes, the Hawaiian Islands were formed.

Above left: Kilauea erupted in 1984, spewing lava from several different parts of the volcano. Above: Children explore the area around Kilauea. The rock has been turned yellow by sulfur in the steam from heated underground water.

Students have come from the Keakealani Outdoor Education Center to the volcano known as Kilauea on a field trip. Their teacher explains to them how volcanic eruptions formed the island they call home. Kilauea is one of five volcanoes that formed the Big Island. The others are Kohala, Hualalai, Mauna Kea, and Mauna Loa. Kilauea and Mauna Loa are the only volcanoes in Hawaii that are still active. Visitors can drive right up to Kilauea's base and see the erupting lava.

Along the coasts of the Hawaiian Islands, ocean waves pound lava rock and slowly break it into sand.

Nothing can stop a moving lava flow. Princess and Terrance learned that when they were small children. Their family has owned land near Kilauea for generations. In 1990, Kilauea had a major eruption, and lava flowed toward their neighborhood. With their family, Princess and Terrance moved to their aunt's house a few miles away and waited there. Days passed, and the lava came closer. It swallowed up some of their neighbors' houses. Then the lava crossed the road and inched onto their land.

Above: *Lava rock in Terrance's yard reminds him and his family how close the lava came to their house.* Right: *Princess holds her niece in front of their house. The road behind them is still covered with lava rock.*

Left: *As a lava flow cools, a crust forms on top. It may still be red-hot liquid underneath.* Below: *Fields of lava rock cover many parts of the Big Island.*

Princess and Terrance and their family prayed that their house would be spared. They believe their prayers were answered, because the lava turned toward the sea just before it reached their house. Two years passed before it was safe for the family to return to their home. After they moved back, the family began selling souvenirs and fruit to visitors who come to see what the lava did.

Hawaii lies 2,500 miles from the nearest land mass. The first plants and animals that lived here had to cross the sea, either in the air or on the water. The smallest seeds may have been carried by the wind or on the feathers of birds. Insects and other small animals most likely arrived on floating plants. During the millions of years since these pioneer life forms first reached Hawaii, they changed very slowly.

Thick rain forest once covered much of the Big Island. Inset: The nene, or Hawaiian goose, is Hawaii's state bird.

The nene is protected by law in Hawaii.

Mongooses are very common in Hawaii. Brought to the Hawaiian Islands by settlers, they have killed large numbers of native animals.

Over time, new species, or kinds, of plants and animals developed from the original species. Many of these new species are unique to the Hawaiian Islands. Over 90 percent of Hawaii's native plants and animals are found nowhere else on Earth. Unfortunately, they are disappearing fast.

Tropical forests once covered much of the Hawaiian Islands. But much of the forest has been replaced by vacation resorts, logging operations, and housing developments. The homes of many forest plants and animals have been destroyed. Half of Hawaii's native bird species are gone. Even the state bird—the nene, or Hawaiian goose—has almost disappeared.

Christopher tosses a rounded stone toward a goal in the ancient Hawaiian game of ulu maika.

Many Hawaiians work hard to save their native plants and animals. Many also work to preserve their native culture. All children take Hawaiian Studies classes in school. At Holualoa Elementary School, Tisa teaches Hawaiian Studies. She shows Christopher how to throw a stone in the ancient Hawaiian game called *ulu maika*. The object of the game is to roll a stone through a goal made of two sticks. If the stone passes between the sticks, players yell *"maikai,"* which means "good" in Hawaiian. If the stone misses, they yell *"auwe,"* which means "oh no."

Once a year, students from six elementary schools on the Big Island come together in Hilo for a Hawaiian games competition. In a game called *palaie,* Dustin swings a ball on a string and tries to catch the ball in a hoop at the end of a stick.

Healani is learning a more recent Hawaiian tradition— playing the ukulele. Portuguese immigrants brought the instrument to Hawaii in the late 1800s. Healani takes ukulele lessons in a Hawaiian immersion program at her school. In this program, classes are taught in the Hawaiian language. Students don't use English at all until the fifth grade.

Healani with her ukulele

Dustin plays palaie *at a Hawaiian games competition.*

Many Hawaiian boys and girls study the Hawaiian dance known as the hula. HopoeLehua enjoys doing traditional hula, or *kahiko,* which is much like the hula danced by early Hawaiians. Traditional hula dancers chant and use hand, body, and face movements to tell a story about legends or historical events.

One of HopoeLehua's favorite dances tells the story of ancient rock carvings called petroglyphs. Petroglyphs are pictures carved on lava rock. Early Hawaiians had no writing, and they used hula dances and petroglyphs to tell stories and share information. Some petroglyphs tell the story of a journey. Others list the members of a family. Still others mark trails or burial sites.

Some Hawaiians dance a modern form of hula known as *auwana.* Oilipiua, Kaui, Alden, Briahni, and Lilinoe are paid to dance *auwana* in a restaurant. Modern hula has lots of rapid hip shaking and is usually accompanied by music.

Top: *Petroglyphs appear at about 135 sites throughout Hawaii. With 70 known sites, the Big Island has the most.* Bottom: *At the Waikoloa Petroglyph Preserve, HopoeLehua dances a hula that tells a story about petroglyphs.*

Oilipiua, Kaui, Alden, Briahni, and Lilinoe dance modern hula on stage at a Big Island restaurant.

In modern-day Hawaii, the word kapu *is sometimes used to mean "keep out."*

KAPU

Beyond this point you may be in danger of being struck by a golf ball. Please return as you came. Mahalo!

This memorial to Captain James Cook overlooks Kealakekua Bay, near the spot where he was killed by Hawaiians during a disagreement in 1778.

In 1778, British sea captain James Cook and his crew became the first Europeans to visit the Hawaiian Islands. During the 1780s, American, British, French, and Russian sailors began active trade with the islands.

Up to this period, many different chiefs ruled the Hawaiian Islands. But in 1795, Kamehameha I, chief of the Big Island, conquered the armies of most other chiefs. He united the islands into a single nation with himself as king.

Before Europeans arrived, Hawaiians had followed their own religion. They worshipped many gods and goddesses. They also followed many different *kapus*, or strict rules. One *kapu* prohibited women from eating certain foods. Another prohibited ordinary people from walking on the same ground as a chief. People who broke a *kapu* were punished and sometimes put to death.

Micah with his parents at the Mokuaikaua Church in Kailua-Kona. The church steeple is the highest structure in town, and boaters use it as a landmark.

Around 1820, under the rule of King Kamehameha II, Hawaiians stopped following the *kapu*s. Missionaries from Europe arrived on the islands at about this time. They converted most Hawaiians to the Christian religion.

Micah and his parents go to a Christian church that stands on the spot where missionaries built Hawaii's first church. Micah's grandfather is the church's pastor.

Ancient Hawaiians called all foreigners *haole*s. Since the first foreigners were white Europeans, the term *haole* is now used to refer to white people. Teighlor is a *haole,* as are about 25 percent of Big Island residents. Another 25 percent are like Grant—part native Hawaiian. Less than 1 percent are pure native Hawaiian.

There aren't many *haole*s at the school where Teighlor and Grant go in the small town of Pahala. Sometimes Teighlor feels a little out of place. But like most *haole*s, she gets along well with her native Hawaiian friends. In fact, Grant's father and Teighlor's mother are dating. Marriages between *haole*s and native Hawaiians are common.

Grant and Teighlor with Teighlor's pet goat

Traditional Hawaiian culture is important to many *haole*s. Some take hula lessons or study the Hawaiian language. Evan wears tattoos of traditional Hawaiian designs. The design of his tattoo comes from Hawaiian tapa cloth. Tapa is made by pounding the bark of the paper mulberry tree and then decorating it. Evan's tattoo is temporary. It will wash off in a few days.

A tattooed tour guide talks about petroglyphs with a group of tourists.

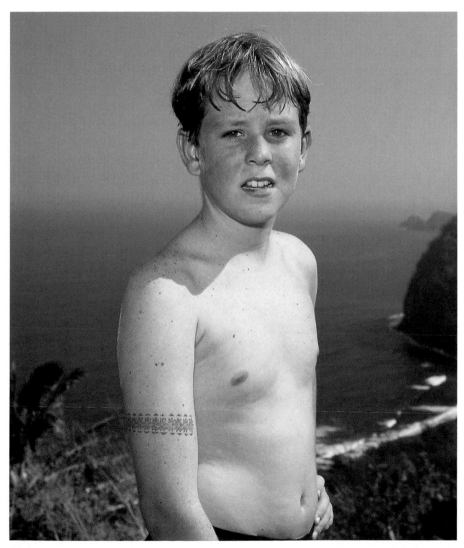

Evan at Pololu Valley

Jeffrey, Eric, and Darin practice a very exciting Hawaiian tradition—surfing, or riding ocean waves to shore. Eric and Darin lie on a short "boogie board." Jeffrey stands and surfs on a longer, more traditional surfboard. The three boys go to the beach every chance they get. They like the biggest waves the best.

Darin with his boogie board and flippers; Eric rides a boogie board; and Jeffrey surfs. Surfing was a popular Hawaiian sport long before Europeans arrived.

These boys use their boogie boards to skim across wet sand at a beach in Kailua-Kona.

Most Hawaiian children learn to surf or use a boogie board. Maile lives on the west coast of the Big Island in Kailua-Kona, the island's second-largest city. Her father, Keoni, teaches her how to surf. Maile's mother and brother surf, too. Sometimes Maile's family travels by plane to the islands of Oahu and Maui to visit relatives. During these visits, the family does lots of surfing. In general, Oahu and Maui have bigger waves than the Big Island.

Keoni teaches Maile how to surf.

Near the beach where Maile learns to surf, Mayra, Antonina, and Kelly collect sea urchins. These small, spine-covered animals live on the ocean floor in five-foot-deep water. To pick up the sea urchins, each girl holds her breath and opens her eyes under water. They plan to show the creatures to Antonina's grandfather, who fishes nearby. Then they will put the sea urchins back in the ocean.

24

Many people go snorkeling or scuba diving to see colorful fish and coral reefs in the ocean surrounding Hawaii. But much sea life can be seen without going into the ocean. At Punaluu Beach, on the Big Island's eastern coast, Jamie and Kristen look for crabs in pools of water along the shore. The day before, they saw a sea turtle come up on the beach to lay its eggs. Hawaiians once hunted sea turtles for their meat, but it is now illegal to harm sea turtles. Whales, seals, coral, and many other kinds of sea life are also now protected in Hawaii.

Jamie and Kristen search for crabs at Punaluu Beach. The beach's black sand was formed from dark lava rock worn down by ocean waves.

Signs at Punaluu Beach warn people to watch for sea turtle nests.

Kiliheaahiah and Holeka with their grandfather Goro

Four miles from Kailua-Kona, on the side of an old volcano, sits the tiny village of Holualoa. Kiliheaahiah and Holeka spend the day here at their grandfather Goro's hotel. Goro takes care of Holeka while his parents work. Today, Goro also watches Kiliheaahiah, because earlier in the day she felt too sick to go to school.

Goro's ancestors are from Japan. During the 1800s, many thousands of immigrants from China, Japan, the Philippines, and Portugal came to the Big Island to work on sugarcane plantations. Sugarcane was once the main product of the state of Hawaii. It still ranks as the state's most important crop.

Many descendants of the early sugarcane workers still live in Hawaii. About 20 percent of people on the Big Island have Japanese ancestry. Japanese culture has greatly influenced life in Hawaii. For example, most Hawaiians take off their shoes when they enter a house, just as people often do in Japan.

Hawaii's tropical climate is good for growing sugarcane.

Like most Hawaiians, Piilani takes off her shoes before going inside.

Staci, Kendall (wearing pink shirt), *and Brandon* (in front) *pick coffee beans.*

The fruit of the coffee plant is called a berry. Each berry contains two coffee beans.

Staci, Kendall, and Brandon have Japanese ancestors too. They live on a small farm down the road from Goro's hotel in Holualoa. Their parents grow squash, papayas, star fruits, pineapples, coconuts, and coffee. The Big Island is one of the few places in the United States where the weather is suitable for growing coffee. Coffee grown on the Big Island is known as Kona coffee.

From August to December, Staci, Kendall, and Brandon spend their weekends helping their parents pick the red coffee beans. Their father owns a coffee shop in Kailua-Kona. The children love to go with their father to the shop, because they usually get to go swimming at a nearby beach.

After they finish picking, Staci climbs a coconut tree in her yard. She pulls and pushes a coconut until it falls to the ground. Kendall looks for chicken eggs. The family's 18 chickens lay their eggs under the coffee plants. The chickens scratch the ground as they search for bugs to eat. This helps the coffee plants because it lets air into the soil.

Kendall shows his father a chicken egg he found under a coffee plant.

Staci climbs a coconut tree to knock down a few coconuts.

Staci, Kendall, and Brandon attend the Holualoa Elementary School, a public school near their home. In Hawaii, public schools are run by the state. In the rest of the United States, public schools are run by local school districts.

As the children arrive at their classroom, Alexandra, Julia, and Joy raise the Hawaiian state flag in the schoolyard. Some Hawaiians fly their flag upside-down to symbolize the Hawaiian sovereignty movement. Many Hawaiians believe that Hawaii should have more independence from the U.S. government because it is so different from other states. Some Hawaiians even want their state to become an independent nation, as it once was.

An upside-down Hawaiian flag symbolizes the Hawaiian sovereignty movement.

Alexandra, Julia, and Joy raise the Hawaiian flag. The eight stripes of red, white, and blue represent the eight major Hawaiian Islands. The British flag appears in the corner and represents the first non-Polynesian people to visit Hawaii.

Hawaii was an independent nation for much of its history. In 1893, a group of American and European businessmen who lived in Hawaii took control of the islands, with the help of the U.S. military.

In 1898, the businessmen persuaded Congress to make Hawaii a U.S. territory. It remained a territory until 1959, when Hawaiians voted to become the 50th state in the United States.

The coast of the Waipio Valley at dawn. Hawaiians take great pride in their state's unique qualities.

Chad works with cattle on his family's ranch.

Much of the northern part of the Big Island is used as ranch land. Chad lives on his family's ranch there. On weekends, he helps his father rope, brand, and drive their cattle. Today, Chad is using a borrowed saddle, and his horse is not yet fully trained. Despite these problems, Chad can do his work because he is a good rider.

Chad is part Hawaiian and part Portuguese. His Portuguese ancestors came to Hawaii to work on the sugarcane plantations in the 1870s. They later bought a small ranch. Many of the Big Island's small ranchers have trouble making a living because they must compete with big ranches. Not far from Chad's home is the vast Parker Ranch. It is one of the largest privately owned ranches in the United States.

James shows off a bonefish he caught near his home in Hilo.

With so many cattle raised on the Big Island, Hawaiians eat lots of beef. They eat fish too, but not as much as they once did. Fish populations have decreased due to over-fishing, and fish are now very expensive.

Many Hawaiians still enjoy fishing on their own. James goes fishing with his parents several times a week. He often catches bonefish, called *oio* in Hawaiian. His father uses *oio* as bait to catch bigger fish.

Daniel (right) *and a friend prepare their sea kayaks for a fishing trip.*

Daniel likes to go fishing too. He lives in Hilo, the Big Island's largest city. He and a friend had planned a fishing trip in their sea kayaks. But soon after they left, the weather turned stormy and they returned to shore. Daniel sees lots of storms, since Hilo lies on the Big Island's rainy east coast. Hilo receives some rain on about 275 days a year. It is known as America's rainiest city.

Lots of rain means lots of flowers, and Hilo is the center of Hawaii's flower industry. Orchids, poinsettias, hibiscus, and other beautiful flowers grow well in Hawaii. Flowers grown in and around Hilo are shipped all over the world.

Cheryl's family owns a flower business near Hilo. They sell flowers, flower arrangements, and traditional Hawaiian necklaces called leis. Leis are made from many different kinds of flowers, leaves, or seashells. Each kind of lei has a special meaning and symbolizes things such as marriage, birth, grief, or death.

Cheryl's mother, Elvira, sells flowers and leis at Hilo's outdoor market. Cheryl helps her mother on Saturdays. When a cruise ship arrives in Hilo, they sell flowers and leis to the passengers.

The canna flower. Beautiful flowers grown in Hawaii are sold all over the world.

Cheryl makes leis from tea leaves at the Hilo market. Tea leaf leis are given for luck.

All kinds of plants grow well in Hawaii's warm, rainy climate, especially on the Big Island's east coast. Papayas, bananas, and oranges are important products of the Big Island.

Cari and Dianne have 15 orange trees in their backyard. They live north of Hilo in the little town of Pepeekeo. They usually go to the beach on weekends. But on Saturdays in October, November, and December, they sell oranges in front of their house. During these months, the oranges become ripe and fall to the ground.

Cari and Dianne sell oranges in their front yard.

Amy has fruit trees in her yard too. She lives in Naalehu, a village in the southern part of the Big Island. Her family grows mandarins, a kind of citrus fruit much like an orange. Mandarins are smaller than oranges and less sweet. Amy's mother soaks them in honey or sugar for a few weeks before she eats them. Amy likes them straight off the tree.

Amy picks mandarins from a tree in her yard.

Most families in Milolii collect rain water in big tanks to use as drinking water. This part of town was built on an old lava flow.

Jessica lives in the village of Milolii on the Big Island's west coast, also known as the Kona Coast. Kona means leeward, or facing away from the wind. High volcanoes in the middle of the island block the winds that bring rain to the east coast. The Kona Coast receives much less rain than the east coast.

On hot, dry days, Jessica cools off in the ocean. She also enjoys going fishing with her family and friends. Jessica's father makes his living by fishing in a traditional Hawaiian way. He feeds the fish pumpkin, avocado, and other vegetables. This brings many fish together to one spot. He feeds the fish for many days, until there are lots of big fish swimming in the area. Then he uses a net to catch them.

For a short time, Jessica and her family lived on the island of Oahu. Her father had a construction job there. Oahu is much smaller than the Big Island, yet three-fourths of Hawaii's 1,160,000 people live there. Jessica and her family are glad to be back on the Big Island. They prefer its open spaces to the crowded island of Oahu.

Jessica fishes with her aunt Sharon and some friends.

Jessica's friends Ikaika, Kainada, and Pono show off some of the fish they caught.

Along the Big Island's northeastern coast, big valleys cut into the hills. Kala and his father live in the largest of these great valleys, the Waipio Valley. Thousands of native Hawaiians once lived here. Now there are fewer than 100 permanent residents.

The Waipio Valley has few modern conveniences. Kala and his father get their electricity from a solar-energy system. Their water flows from a stream through a pipe to their home. To enter and leave the valley, they must walk or get a ride in a four-wheel-drive car or truck.

The Waipio Valley is about a mile wide and bordered by cliffs up to 2,000 feet high.

Kala

Like most people in the Waipio Valley, Kala's father is a taro farmer. Taro plants are grown in knee-high water. After the plants are ripe, the roots can be mashed into a nutritious, pasty food called poi. Hawaiians once ate lots of poi. But sugarcane growers have taken most of the water from streams that flow into the Waipio Valley. With less water to flood their fields, most of the valley's taro farmers went out of business and had to move elsewhere.

Most families in the Waipio Valley grow taro plants.

Kala sometimes meets tourists on the beach near his home. Tourists are called *malihini*s in Hawaiian. Tourism is the state of Hawaii's biggest source of income. Most *malihini*s stay on the island of Oahu, but many visit the Big Island too. They come to play in the ocean, see the volcanoes, and enjoy the beautiful scenery.

Near their campsite, Carlos, Chase, Nancy, and Canyon prepare to walk across the Waipio River.

Canyon watches big waves crash against Waipio Valley Beach.

Canyon and Chase live in Montana. They met Kala while on a camping vacation with their family in the Waipio Valley. They carried in food, tents, and sleeping bags and set up camp in the trees facing the ocean.

Later, the boys decided to build a small hut out of sticks and palm tree branches. Kala suggested that they cover the roof with small twigs from the forest floor to keep out the rain. Chase and his father spent the night in the hut. They enjoyed falling asleep to the sound of ocean waves.

Chase and Canyon place small twigs on the hut they built.

The Big Island's population is growing, and tourism brings more and more people every year. With more people, the Big Island has had to produce more electricity. A new geothermal power plant was recently built near Hilo. The plant makes electricity from the energy in underground steam.

This Hawaiian resort has a dolphin pool for its guests.

This resort hotel was built near the north end of Hapuna Beach State Park.

Waiala, Heather, and Mariah outside the geothermal power plant near their home

Sheena, Kahealani, and Nicole enjoy playing volleyball at Hapuna Beach State Park.

When the steam is piped to the surface, harmful gases are sometimes also released. Waiala, Heather, and Mariah live near the plant. Their parents think gases from the plant may have made the girls sick. Other people say that the power plant is not the cause. This controversy is just one example of the issues Hawaiians face as population and tourism increase.

To accommodate tourists, more and more resorts and hotels are being built on the Big Island. Some people welcome these developments, which bring jobs to the area. Others worry that all the new buildings will spoil the land's natural beauty.

Hawaiians have a deep *aloha aina*, or love of the land. They want to preserve the Big Island's beauty for the future. The children of Hawaii will have to face the challenge of balancing the needs of the modern world with their love of the land.

More about Hawaii

How big is the Big Island of Hawaii?

The Big Island has an area of 4,038 square miles. It is about the size of Delaware and Rhode Island combined.

How did Hawaii get its name?

One ancient Hawaiian legend says that the Hawaiian Islands were named after a Polynesian chief called Hawaii-loa. This chief is said to have led the Polynesians to the islands. Another explanation is that early Polynesian settlers named the island after their homeland in the western Pacific Ocean, which had been called Hawaiki.

How many people live in Hawaii?

About 1.2 million people live in the state of Hawaii. Of those, about one-tenth, or 131,000 people, live on the Big Island.

What else is the Big Island known for?

The inactive volcano Mauna Kea is the highest mountain in Hawaii, at 13,796 feet above sea level. Some say it's the highest mountain in the world, because when measured from its base on the ocean floor, it rises up to 33,476 feet. Mauna Kea and the active volcano Mauna Loa cover most of the Big Island. The top of Mauna Kea is known as the best place in the world for astronomical observation. Some of the biggest telescopes in the world are found there.

Pronunciation Guide

The Hawaiian Language

The Hawaiian alphabet has only 12 letters: *a, e, h, i, k, l, m, n, o, p, u,* and *w.* Every letter of a word is sounded, and all syllables and words end in vowels. The accent usually falls on the next to last syllable.

aloha ah-LOH-hah
haole HOW-lay
Hawaii huh-WAH-yee
Hilo HEE-loh
Holualoa hoh-loo-ah-LOH-ah
hula HOO-lah
Kailua-Kona kie-LOO-ah-KOH-nah
Kamehameha kah-may-hah-MAY-hah
kapu KAH-poo
Kilauea kee-lau-AY-ah
lei LAY
mahalo mah-HAH-loh
malihini mah-lee-HEE-nee
Mauna Kea MOW-nah KAY-ah
Mauna Loa MOW-nah LOH-ah
Milolii mee-loh-LEE-yee
Naalehu nah-ah-LAY-hoo
nene nay-nay
Oahu oh-WAH-hoo
Pepeekeo pay-pay-KAY-oh
petroglyph PEH-truh-glif
Polynesia pahl-uh-NEE-zhuh
Punaluu poo-nah-LOO-oo
ukulele yoo-kuh-LAY-lee
ulu maika oo-loo mah-EE-kah
Waipio Valley why-pee-oh VA-lee

This Hawaiian-style graffiti was made with white coral rocks on black lava rock.

Index